THE LITTLE POETRY BOOK ABOUT LOVING YORKSHIRE TERRIERS

The Little Poetry Book about Loving Yorkshire Terriers

Walter the Educator

SKB

Silent King Books

dedicated to all the Yorkshire Terrier
lovers across the world

CONTENTS

WHY I CREATED THIS BOOK?

Creating a poetry book about loving Yorkshire Terriers was a unique and heartfelt endeavor for several reasons. Firstly, Yorkshire Terriers are beloved pets known for their charm, loyalty, and adorable nature. They inspire a deep affection and connection in their owners, making them a perfect subject for poetry.

Furthermore, poetry allows for the expression of emotions and the exploration of themes such as love, companionship, and the beauty of nature. By focusing on Yorkshire Terriers, the poems can capture the joys and challenges of having these delightful creatures in one's life.

Additionally, a poetry book about Yorkshire Terriers can serve as a tribute to these wonderful dogs, celebrating their unique personalities, quirks, and the special bond they share with their human companions. It can also be an opportunity to educate and raise awareness about the breed, its history, and the importance of responsible pet ownership.

Overall, creating a poetry book about loving Yorkshire Terriers enables the expression of love, admiration, and appreciation for these charming dogs while providing an avenue for creative exploration and connection with dog lovers.

ONE

ENDLESSLY FLOWS

In a world of wagging tails and charms,
Where tiny paws hold hearts in their arms,
There exists a breed so small, so bright,
Yorkshire Terriers, a pure delight.

With fur in shades of gold and blue,
Eyes that sparkle, hearts so true,
Yorkies prance with grace and pride,
Their love, a joy that can't be denied.

In their tiny frames, courage resides,
Their spirit fierce, like a lion that strides,
Though small in stature, they stand tall,
Yorkies conquer hearts, one and all.

Their loyalty, a bond that won't sever,
They'll follow you, forever and ever,
Yorkies bring laughter, love, and cheer,
Their presence fills every moment near.

They curl up on laps in peaceful repose,
Their love, like a river, endlessly flows,
With a wag of their tail, they'll steal your heart,
Yorkies, a masterpiece of canine art.
So cherish these creatures, gentle and kind,
Yorkshire Terriers, a treasure you'll find,
For in their love, there's magic untold,
A love so pure, worth more than gold.

TWO

YORKSHIRE SOULS

In a world of boundless love and joy,
Where Yorkshire Terriers bring delight,
Their tiny frames, filled with grace,
Captivate hearts both day and night.
    With eyes that gleam like precious jewels,
And coats of silk, so soft and fine,
They prance with elegance and poise,
A breed that's truly quite divine.
    Their loyalty knows no bounds,
With hearts so pure, they never waver,
Always by your side, they'll stay,
A faithful friend, your trust they savor.
    Their playful nature brings such mirth,
Bounding through fields, tails held high,
Their zest for life, infectious and bright,
They chase away every worry and sigh.

In their eyes, you'll find a love so deep,
A bond that time can never sever,
With every wag of their tail,
They show you their love, forever.
So let us celebrate these Yorkshire souls,
With their spirit bold and true,
For in their presence, life is complete,
A love that's cherished, through and through.

THREE

SPIRIT SO GRAND

In fields of gold, a Yorkshire Terrier plays,
With eyes so bright, like diamonds in sun's rays.
A tiny frame, but a heart so bold,
A love like this, never grows old.
    With every wag of their tail, joy they bring,
A bond so strong, like an eternal spring.
Their loyalty, a gift bestowed,
A love like this, forever aglow.
    Their silky coat, so soft to touch,
A cuddle, a snuggle, it means so much.
In their presence, worries fade away,
A love like this, forever will stay.
    Their playfulness, a joy to behold,
Bringing laughter, filling hearts with gold.
In their eyes, a spark of pure delight,
A love like this, never takes flight.

Though small in size, their spirit so grand,
Their love, a treasure in life's vast land.
In every moment, their love's on display,
A love like this, never fades away.
So let us cherish these furry friends,
Their love, a bond that never ends.
For in their presence, we find pure bliss,
A love like this, forever amiss.

FOUR

ONE OF A KIND

In the land where terriers bark,
There's a breed that leaves a mark,
With fur of gold, so silky fine,
A Yorkshire Terrier, divine.

Their eyes, like gems, sparkle bright,
Reflecting love, pure and light,
Their tiny paws, so dainty and neat,
Graceful dancers, light on their feet.

With hearts so big, beyond their size,
They fill our days with joy and surprise,
Their loyalty, a treasure untold,
A bond with humans, strong and bold.

They prance and play with endless glee,
Their spirit wild, forever free,
Yet in their eyes, a gentle gaze,
A love that lasts through endless days.

Their barks, like music, fill the air,
A symphony of love and care,
Their presence brings a warmth so true,
A Yorkshire Terrier, I adore you.

So let us celebrate their charm,
Their love that keeps us safe and warm,
For in their company, we find,
A love that's rare and one of a kind.

FIVE

SPARKLE OF DELIGHT

In fields of gold, where sunlight gleams,
A Yorkshire Terrier, the dog of dreams.
With eyes so bright, and a heart so pure,
A love for this breed, forever endure.
    Their tiny frames, with grace they move,
Bringing joy and laughter, they never fail to prove.
Their silky coats, a shade of gold,
Soft as moonlight, a beauty to behold.
    With every wag of their dainty tail,
They fill our hearts, they never fail.
Their loyalty, unwavering and true,
A Yorkshire Terrier, forever we'll pursue.
    In their presence, worries fade away,
Their playful antics, a delightful display.
From cuddles on laps, to walks in the park,
The love of a Yorkie, a glowing spark.

In their eyes, a sparkle of delight,
A bond so strong, an eternal light.
As they snuggle close, by our side,
With Yorkshire Terriers, love abides.

So let us cherish these furry friends,
Their love and companionship, it never ends.
For in their presence, our hearts are whole,
A Yorkshire Terrier, a treasure to behold.

SIX

BOND UNBREAKABLE

In dreams they roam, these dogs of grace,
With bright eyes and pure hearts they chase.
Yorkshire Terriers, small in size,
But mighty in spirit, a joyful surprise.

Their silky coats, like golden thread,
Flowing with elegance as they tread.
With every step, a dance so light,
They bring a spark, a radiant delight.

Loyal and true, their hearts so pure,
Yorkshire Terriers, forever secure.
They fill our lives with boundless love,
Sent from the heavens, a gift from above.

Through rough terrain, they bravely go,
Their spirits strong, their love does grow.
In our darkest hours, they bring the light,
Guiding us through the depths of night.

A bond unbreakable, forged from the start,
Love that transcends, straight to the heart.
Yorkshire Terriers, our faithful friends,
With them, the journey never ends.
So let us cherish these dogs so dear,
For they bring us joy, year after year.
In their presence, our souls take flight,
A love so pure, shining ever bright.

SEVEN

A TREASURE UNTOLD

In realms of joy, where love takes flight,
There dwells a breed, full of delight.
With fur so fine, as golden rays,
Yorkshire Terriers, my heart obeys.
With eyes that shimmer, like twinkling stars,
They steal my soul, no matter how far.
Their tiny paws, so full of grace,
Leave traces of love in every place.
Their spirit, bold, like a lion's roar,
Yet gentle as a whisper on the shore.
In their embrace, I find solace deep,
As they fill my world, in slumber's keep.
Their loyalty, unwavering and true,
A love so pure, it breaks through.
Yorkies, companions, forever by my side,
In their presence, my heart can't hide.

No matter the size, their love is grand,
A bond that's forged, no one can withstand.
Yorkshire Terriers, a treasure untold,
In their love, I find pure gold.

EIGHT

HEARTS SAIL

In a world of wagging tails and charm,
Where tiny paws leave an indelible mark,
There's a breed that steals hearts with ease,
Yorkshire Terriers, small but mighty in degrees.
With coats of silk, shining bright,
Their eyes filled with curiosity and delight,
These tiny dogs, a bundle of joy,
Bring happiness and love, no ploy.
Their playful antics and endless energy,
Fill our lives with boundless glee,
From morning walks to playful games,
Yorkies bring light, like flickering flames.
Their loyalty knows no bounds,
In their presence, love resounds,
With every wag of their little tail,
They make our hearts sail.

Through life's ups and downs they stand,
A faithful companion, a helping hand,
They bring comfort in times of strife,
A Yorkshire Terrier, a friend for life.
So let us celebrate these furry friends,
Whose love and devotion never ends,
With their presence, life's a treasure,
Loving Yorkshire Terriers, beyond measure.

NINE

SPECIAL BOND

In the land where terriers roam,
Yorkshire's heart finds its home.
With a spirit so fierce yet tender,
A love for Yorkies I'll forever surrender.
  Their tiny frames, oh so petite,
Yet their presence fills my heart's retreat.
Their silky coats, a sight to behold,
Like golden threads spun from stories untold.
  With eyes that gleam like diamonds bright,
They bring joy to even the darkest night.
Their boundless energy, a playful delight,
Bringing laughter and smiles, oh what a sight!
  Loving Yorkies is a special bond,
A love that's true, a love so fond.
In their company, worries fade away,
As they fill our lives with endless play.

Their loyalty, unwavering and strong,
A love that lasts, a bond lifelong.
In their eyes, a love that never wanes,
A love that surpasses all earthly gains.
So here's to Yorkies, small and grand,
Capturing hearts with their charm so grand.
A love so pure, it knows no measure,
Loving Yorkshire Terriers, a lifelong treasure.

TEN

CONSTANT SOURCE OF LOVE

In a world where hearts find solace,
Amidst the chaos and the strife,
There exists a breed so precious,
A Yorkshire Terrier, full of life.

With silky coat of golden hue,
And eyes that sparkle like the stars,
A loyal friend, forever true,
They'll brighten up life's darkest scars.

Small in size, but mighty in heart,
They bring joy with every wagging tail,
Their love, an art, an exquisite art,
That fills our lives without fail.

Their playful antics, a true delight,
As they prance and dance with glee,

Their presence brings warmth, day and night,
A Yorkshire Terrier's love, pure and free.
    Through years and seasons they remain,
A constant source of love and cheer,
In our hearts, they forever reign,
These tiny guardians, we hold dear.
    So let us celebrate their grace,
And cherish every precious day,
For in their eyes, we find a place,
A love that never fades away.
    Oh, Yorkshire Terriers, we adore,
Your spirit, fierce, your love, profound,
Forever in our hearts, forevermore,
With you, our happiness knows no bound.

ELEVEN

NO MATTER THE SIZE

In the realm of canine grace,
A breed so small, yet full of grace,
Yorkshire Terriers, a sight to behold,
With hearts of gold and stories untold.
    Their silky coats, a shimmering hue,
In shades of silver and deepest blue,
Eyes that sparkle like diamonds rare,
With a mischievous glint and a loving stare.
    With each wag of their tiny tail,
They bring joy that will never fail,
Their loyalty, steadfast and true,
Yorkshire Terriers, we cherish you.
    In their tiny frames, courage resides,
Fearless spirits, they won't hide,
They'll defend and protect, no matter the size,
Yorkshire Terriers, a noble surprise.

Their playful nature, a constant delight,
Bounding with energy, morning to night,
They'll chase their toys with fervent glee,
Yorkshire Terriers, forever carefree.

But beneath their playful demeanor,
Lies a love that's even sweeter,
Loyal companions, by our side,
Yorkshire Terriers, our hearts confide.

So let us celebrate this breed so dear,
Their love and joy, forever near,
Yorkshire Terriers, forever adored,
In our hearts, you are forever stored.

TWELVE

PRECIOUS SOULS

In a world of canine charm and grace,
There's a breed that holds a special place.
With silky coats of golden hue,
Yorkshire Terriers, so small but true.

Their eyes, like gems, sparkle and gleam,
Reflecting love in a gentle beam.
Their hearts, so big, beat pure and strong,
A loyal companion all life long.

With paws that dance and tails that wag,
They brighten days and never lag.
Their playful spirit knows no bounds,
Bounding through life with joyful sounds.

In their presence, worries disappear,
As they fill our hearts with love so dear.
Their tiny frames hold endless joy,
A love that nothing can destroy.

And when the moon paints the sky above,
They curl beside us, filled with love.
Their warmth, a comfort, through the night,
Yorkshire Terriers, a true delight.
So let us cherish their precious souls,
And honor the love that truly unfolds.
For in their eyes, we find the key,
To a love that sets our spirits free.

THIRTEEN

PURE PERFECTION

In fields of gold, a Yorkshire Terrier prances free,
A tiny soul with boundless love, as far as the eye can see.
With silky coat of caramel and ebony,
This little pup brings joy, a lively symphony.

With eyes so bright, filled with unconditional affection,
A Yorkshire Terrier's love is a true reflection.
Their playful spirit dances, a joyous connection,
A companion that fills your heart with pure perfection.

In their tiny paws, a world of love they hold,
A Yorkshire Terrier, more precious than gold.
Their loyalty and devotion, a story untold,
A love so deep, it never grows old.

Through gardens they frolic, tails wagging with glee,

A Yorkshire Terrier, a friend to set your heart free.
With every gentle lick and cuddle, you can see,
That loving a Yorkshire Terrier is where happiness will be.

So let us celebrate these furry friends so dear,
The Yorkshire Terrier, a companion so sincere.
Their love transcends all boundaries, crystal clear,
For in their presence, all worries disappear.

In the embrace of a Yorkshire Terrier's love,
Life's troubles seem to fade, like a gentle dove.
So cherish these little souls, sent from above,
For loving a Yorkshire Terrier is pure, unwavering love.

FOURTEEN

SMALL, YET BOLD

In a world of wagging tails and boundless joy,
There thrives a breed that's small, yet bold - the York-
shire Terrier.
With fur of gold, like sunlit rays,
They captivate our hearts in countless ways.

Their tiny paws tread with grace and poise,
As they explore the world with innocent eyes.
Their presence brings warmth, a love so pure,
Yorkshire Terriers, forever we'll adore.

With hearts so big, though bodies quite small,
They conquer obstacles, standing tall.
Their loyalty never falters, forever true,
A Yorkshire Terrier's love, a treasure to pursue.

Their playful spirit, a constant delight,
They chase their tails in pure delight.

With each wag of their tail, a smile is born,
Their happiness infectious, from dusk till dawn.
    They cuddle close, a comforting embrace,
A Yorkshire Terrier's love, a haven in any place.
In their gentle gaze, kindness resides,
A love that endures, forever abides.
    Their barks may be mighty, their voices strong,
But their love for us, everlasting and long.
They bring us joy, day after day,
A Yorkshire Terrier's love, here to stay.
    So let us cherish these furry friends,
The ones who love us, until the end.
For in the heart of a Yorkshire Terrier,
We find a love that can never falter or vary.

FIFTEEN

SILKY GOLD

In a realm where love abounds,
A Yorkshire Terrier's grace resounds.
With eyes so bright, like stars above,
Their presence fills our hearts with love.

Their tiny frame, a joy to behold,
Wrapped in fur of silky gold.
With each playful leap and bound,
They bring happiness all around.

Their loyalty knows no bounds,
A faithful friend, always around.
In cold winter nights, by the fire's glow,
They warm our hearts, their love does show.

With a wag of their tail, a gentle lick,
They bring smiles that heal and stick.
In their eyes, a spark of mischief gleams,
Chasing dreams, like fleeting beams.

Their barks, a symphony of delight,
Protecting our homes day and night.
Yet, in their heart, a gentle soul,
A love that makes us feel whole.
Oh, Yorkshire Terrier, precious and rare,
With you, life becomes a joyful affair.
In your presence, our spirits soar,
A love for you forevermore.

SIXTEEN

EYES LIKE GEMS

In a realm of boundless joy and bliss,
Where Yorkshire Terriers dance and kiss,
A love so pure, it can't be contained,
A devotion that forever remains.

With eyes like gems, so bright and clear,
They hold a love that's always near,
Their tiny paws, a gentle touch,
Their loyalty, it means so much.

With silky coats, flowing in the breeze,
They bring a smile, a sense of ease,
Their playful nature, a joyful delight,
They fill our days and dreams at night.

In their presence, worries fade,
As their love, like sunlight, cascades,
They warm our hearts with every wag,
A love so deep, it's hard to lag.

They teach us lessons, simple and true,
To cherish love, in all that we do,
To be loyal, faithful, and kind,
With a Yorkshire Terrier, love we find.

So let us bask in their gentle grace,
And cherish every loving embrace,
For in their eyes, we see a love so rare,
Yorkshire Terriers, beyond compare.

SEVENTEEN

RAY OF LIGHT

In fields of green, a pup so small,
With silky hair, a bouncing ball,
A Yorkshire Terrier, full of grace,
A loving heart, a joyful face.
    With eyes that twinkle, bright and clear,
A loyal friend, forever near,
Their tiny frames, so full of zest,
A furry bundle, love at its best.
    In every wag, a tale untold,
Of love and joy, a story unfold,
Their gentle souls, like angels' wings,
Bring warmth and happiness, life's simple things.
    With every bark, a song they sing,
A melody of love they bring,
Their loyal hearts, forever true,
A Yorkshire Terrier, I adore you.

With playful hops and lively prance,
They fill our lives with sweet romance,
Their presence, like a ray of light,
Guiding us through both day and night.

In cuddles shared and kisses bestowed,
A Yorkshire Terrier, our hearts have sowed,
A bond so deep, it can't be broken,
Love unspoken, yet never unspoken.

So let us cherish these furry friends,
For in their love, our hearts transcend,
With Yorkshire Terriers by our side,
Love and joy, forever abide.

EIGHTEEN

BRAVE AND BOLD

In a world of love, so tender and true,
Yorkshire Terriers, my heart belongs to you.
With tiny paws and eyes so bright,
You fill my days with pure delight.
    Your silky coat, a shimmering gold,
A regal presence, both brave and bold.
You prance and strut with utmost grace,
A miniature powerhouse, full of charm and grace.
    Your loyalty, unwavering and strong,
Fills my heart with a joyful song.
With each wag of your tail, my spirits rise,
A love so pure, it reaches the skies.
    Your playful antics, a daily delight,
Chasing balls, bringing laughter to life.
You snuggle close, seeking warmth and care,
A constant reminder, love is everywhere.

In your eyes, I see a world so bright,
A bond so strong, it feels just right.
You are more than just a pet to me,
A cherished companion, forever to be.
   Yorkshire Terriers, oh how I adore,
Your presence in my life, I can't ignore.
In your tiny frame, a love so grand,
A testament to the wonders of this land.
   So here's to the Yorkshire Terriers so dear,
A breed of love, nothing to fear.
Forever in my heart, you'll forever stay,
Yorkshire Terriers, my love for you will never fade away.

NINETEEN

SKIES ABOVE

In fields of gold, a tiny charm,
A Yorkshire Terrier, so full of charm.
With silky fur and eyes so bright,
A little bundle of pure delight.
    With a heart so big, and love so pure,
A Yorkshire Terrier, forever sure.
In every wag of their happy tail,
A love so strong, it will never fail.
    Their tiny paws and playful ways,
Bring joy to every passing day.
With loyalty and devotion strong,
A Yorkshire Terrier, where you belong.
    They may be small in stature, it's true,
But their love for you is always true.
They'll cuddle close, right by your side,
A Yorkshire Terrier, your faithful guide.

So let us celebrate their love,
With open hearts, like skies above.
For in their presence, we find pure bliss,
A Yorkshire Terrier's love, forever amiss.

TWENTY

EVERY STRIDE

In a land of Yorkshire charm,
Where tiny paws and hearts are warm,
There roams a breed so full of grace,
Yorkshire Terriers, in this enchanting place.

With eyes like stars, so bright and clear,
They fill our lives with love and cheer,
Their silky coats, a sight to behold,
Shimmering like threads of purest gold.

In their presence, our worries fade away,
Yorkshire Terriers make our hearts sway,
With playful antics and joyful barks,
They light up our days, like shooting sparks.

Their loyalty knows no bounds,
As they follow us around, without any bounds,
They're always there, by our side,
Through every storm and every stride.

Their tiny frames hold hearts so big,
Yorkshire Terriers, a love so deep and trig,
They bring us joy, they bring us peace,
Their love for us will never cease.
So let us celebrate these little creatures,
Yorkshire Terriers, our heart's best features,
For in their love, we find pure bliss,
A love that we'll forever reminisce.

TWENTY-ONE

LOVE OVERFLOWS

In a world of boundless joy and delight,
Where tiny paws dance, so fluffy and bright,
There's a breed that captures hearts with its grace,
The Yorkshire Terrier, with love in its trace.

With eyes so deep, like pools of purest gold,
And a coat so silky, a sight to behold,
They prance and they play, with spirits so high,
Yorkies fill our lives with endless sky.

Their love is fierce, their loyalty true,
Yorkshire Terriers, a friend through and through,
They cuddle and snuggle, warming our souls,
With hearts so big, as love overflows.

They may be small, but their love is grand,
Yorkies bring smiles to every hand,
They chase away sorrows, they heal every pain,
In their presence, life's never the same.

With each wag of their tail, a love story unfolds,
Yorkshire Terriers, the purest of gold,
They light up our lives, like stars in the night,
Guiding us through darkness, with love as their light.

So let us cherish them, these tiny wonders,
Yorkies, the heart stealers, the love hunters,
For in their embrace, we find solace and glee,
Loving Yorkshire Terriers, forever they'll be.

TWENTY-TWO

SWEETEST CONNECTION

In a world of boundless joy and cheer,
There's a breed that brings hearts near,
With a spirit so bright, so full of glee,
Yorkshire Terriers, they enchant me.

Their tiny frame, like a delicate art,
Conceals a fire burning in their heart,
With eyes that twinkle, mischief in their gaze,
They fill our lives with love's sweet blaze.

Their silky coat, like spun gold,
Cascades gracefully, a story untold,
With each gentle stroke, a bond is made,
A love that will never fade.

Yorkies, loyal and true,
With you, every day feels new,

In your presence, troubles disappear,
Replaced by love, pure and clear.

Though small in size, their spirit is grand,
A courageous soul, they proudly stand,
Protecting their loved ones, come what may,
Faithful companions, guiding the way.

In their presence, laughter abounds,
Through life's ups and downs,
Their playful antics, a source of delight,
A Yorkshire Terrier, a pure delight.

So let us celebrate these furry friends,
Whose love knows no bounds, no ends,
For in their eyes, we find a reflection,
Of love's purest, sweetest connection.

Oh, Yorkshire Terrier, you bring such grace,
A love that time cannot erase,
Forever cherished, forever adored,
In our hearts, you are forever adored.

TWENTY-THREE

BREED DIVINE

In a world of boundless love, there's a breed divine,
With spirited hearts and eyes that brightly shine.
Yorkshire Terriers, small but mighty they stand,
With silky coats and paws that leave no trace in sand.

Their presence, a joy that words cannot convey,
A companion so loyal, by your side they'll stay.
Their playful antics, a source of endless delight,
From dusk till dawn, they chase their dreams in flight.

With hearts full of devotion, they'll follow your lead,
A friend in need, their love you'll never need to plead.
In your darkest hours, they'll be a beacon of light,
Their love, a balm that brings comfort day and night.

Their tiny frames hold a spirit so grand,
With courage and determination, they take a stand.

In their eyes, you'll glimpse a universe of affection,
A connection so pure, a bond without rejection.
Their presence brings warmth to even the coldest days,
Their wagging tails, a symphony of joyful praise.
In their company, troubles seem to fade away,
Yorkshire Terriers, the sunshine in life's gray.
So let us celebrate these canine wonders with glee,
Yorkshire Terriers, a gift to humanity, you see.
Their love transcends boundaries, it knows no end,
A testament to the power of a furry friend.
In the realm of adoration, they reign supreme,
Yorkshire Terriers, the stuff of every dog lover's dream.
So cherish their love, hold them close to your heart,
For in their tiny souls, a love story shall start.

TWENTY-FOUR

DOGS SO DEAR

In the realm of pets, a breed so fine,
A Yorkshire Terrier, a love divine.
With grace and charm, they steal your heart,
These tiny wonders, a breed apart.
Their silky coats, like golden thread,
Flowing and shimmering, oh so well-bred.
Their eyes so bright, with a playful gaze,
Filled with love that never decays.
With every step, they prance and strut,
Confident and bold, never a mutt.
Their loyalty unmatched, a true friend,
A Yorkshire Terrier, till the end.
In their presence, joy fills the air,
Their presence, a remedy for despair.
They bring laughter, love, and delight,
A Yorkshire Terrier, a pure delight.

Their tiny paws, so delicate and small,
Leave imprints on hearts, the greatest of all.
With every wag of their tail, pure bliss,
In their company, there's nothing amiss.
So let us celebrate these dogs so dear,
Yorkshire Terriers, forever near.
For in their love, we find solace and glee,
A Yorkshire Terrier, a true beauty.
In their eyes, a world of devotion,
A Yorkshire Terrier, a heartfelt emotion.
So let us cherish these dogs so dear,
For they bring joy and love, year after year.

TWENTY-FIVE

TWINKLING STARS

In a world of joy and wagging tails,
Where love takes the shape of Yorkshire Terriers,
With eyes so bright, like twinkling stars,
They steal our hearts, no matter who we are.
Their tiny paws, so delicate and sweet,
A playful spirit that can't be beat,
With fur like silk, so soft to touch,
They bring us happiness, oh, so much.
In their presence, worries fade away,
As they bring laughter and brighten each day,
Their loyalty knows no bounds,
A bond so strong, forever profound.
With every bark, they fill the air,
Spreading love and joy without a care,
Their tiny bodies hold a soul so vast,
An unconditional love that will forever last.

Oh, Yorkshire Terriers, you bring us bliss,
A love so pure, we cannot resist,
In your eyes, we find a love so true,
Our hearts forever belong to you

TWENTY-SIX

WON'T EXPIRE

In a world of joy and wagging tails,
Where love resides, where hope prevails,
There lives a breed, so small and bright,
A Yorkshire Terrier, a pure delight.
With fur as soft as silky dreams,
Eyes that sparkle like moonlit streams,
A heart so big, though small in size,
They fill our days with endless skies.
Their presence brings a touch of grace,
As they prance with elegance and embrace,
Each step they take, a dance so dear,
Bringing laughter and cheer, so clear.
They cuddle close, a warming touch,
Their loyalty, it means so much,
A friend for life, through thick and thin,
A Yorkshire Terrier, a love within.

Their playful spirit, a joyful song,
They chase their tails, all day long,
With boundless energy, they never tire,
Their love, a flame that won't expire.

In their eyes, a love so pure,
A bond that's everlasting, sure,
In every moment, they remind,
That love, in small things, we can find.

So let us cherish these furry friends,
For love and joy, they always send,
A Yorkshire Terrier, a love so true,
Forever grateful, we are to you.

TWENTY-SEVEN

WAGGING TAILS

In lands where love for tiny paws reside,
A Yorkshire Terrier, so full of pride.
With eyes that twinkle, like stars in the sky,
A heart so loyal, it will never deny.
  Their coats, like silk, that glistens in the sun,
A charm that captivates, second to none.
Their petite frames, with grace they prance,
A bundle of joy, a delightful dance.
  With wagging tails and constant cheer,
Yorkies bring happiness, oh so near.
Their barks, a melody, so sweet and clear,
Filling our lives with love, year after year.
  They cuddle close, warming our hearts,
A love so pure, it never departs.
Through ups and downs, they're always there,
A Yorkshire Terrier, beyond compare.

So let us celebrate these furry friends,
Whose love and loyalty knows no ends.
For in their presence, we find solace true,
Oh, Yorkshire Terrier, we cherish you!

TWENTY-EIGHT

SPIRIT IS FIERCE

In a realm of boundless charm and grace,
Where love takes form in a tiny space,
There dwells a breed so precious, so dear,
The Yorkshire Terrier, forever near.
With eyes that gleam like stars at night,
And a heart that radiates pure delight,
Their silky coat, a cascade of gold,
A testament to a love untold.
In each wag of their tail, a world of devotion,
Their presence a balm, a soothing potion,
With every step, they conquer hearts,
Their love, a masterpiece of fine arts.
Their spirit is fierce, their loyalty true,
A Yorkshire Terrier, a friend so few,
They may be small in stature and size,
But their love fills the world, reaching the skies.

Through laughter and tears, they stand by our side,
In joy and in sorrow, their love won't hide,
They teach us to cherish the simple things,
To find beauty in life's small offerings.
So let us celebrate the Yorkshire's embrace,
Their love, a beacon in every place,
For in their eyes, we find a love so rare,
A Yorkshire Terrier, forever we'll care.

TWENTY-NINE

LOVE SO TRUE

In fields of green and skies so blue,
There's a love that's pure and forever true.
A Yorkshire Terrier, small and sweet,
With a heart of gold, their love complete.
With eyes so bright, like stars at night,
They bring joy and warmth, a pure delight.
Their tiny paws, so dainty and fine,
Leave footprints of love, like a precious sign.
Their silky fur, a coat so grand,
A touch so soft, like velvet sand.
They prance and play with endless glee,
Their spirit infectious, for all to see.
In their tiny frame, a spirit so bold,
A love so fierce, a story untold.
They curl up close, a loyal friend,
A love that's boundless, with no end.

They bring laughter and cuddles, day and night,
Their presence a comfort, a guiding light.
Through thick and thin, they'll always be near,
A Yorkshire Terrier, forever dear.
So let us celebrate this love so true,
For Yorkshire Terriers, and all they do.
Their love is boundless, their hearts so pure,
A love that's cherished, forevermore.

THIRTY

CANNOT ERASE

In a world of fur so fine and neat,
There dwells a breed so small and sweet.
With eyes that shimmer, bright and clear,
The Yorkshire Terrier, so dear.
　　Their tiny paws dance on the ground,
A playful spirit, forever unbound.
With silky hair, like golden thread,
They steal our hearts, where love is spread.
　　With hearts so big, beyond their size,
They fill our days with endless skies.
Their love is pure, their loyalty true,
Yorkshire Terriers, we adore you.
　　Their presence brings a joyful light,
A constant source of pure delight.
They cuddle close, a warm embrace,
A love that time cannot erase.

In gardens green, they prance and play,
Their barks like music, a joyful ballet.
With every wag of their curly tail,
Yorkshire Terriers, you never fail.

In our lives, you hold a special place,
With love and joy, your gentle grace.
Forever loyal, forever kind,
A Yorkshire Terrier, a love we find.

So let us cherish, with hearts aflame,
These little beings, without a name.
For in their eyes, a love so true,
Yorkshire Terriers, we love you.

THIRTY-ONE

FEARLESSLY EMBARK

In the realm of canine charm, a breed so fine,
Yorkshire Terriers, with hearts that brightly shine.
Their silky coats, a tapestry of gold and blue,
Captivating hearts with every step they do.
   Their eyes, like pools of liquid warmth and grace,
Reflecting love, tenderness in every trace.
A playful spirit, joyful in their every way,
Yorkies bring laughter, brightening each day.
   With tiny paws and wagging tails held high,
They prance and dance beneath the open sky.
Their loyalty, a bond that's eternally strong,
Yorkshire Terriers, a love that's never wrong.
   In grand adventures, they fearlessly embark,
With courage unmatched, they illuminate the dark.
Their presence, a constant source of comfort and joy,
Yorkies, the precious gems that none can destroy.

In every cuddle, a symphony of love they share,
Nuzzling close, their affection beyond compare.
Yorkshire Terriers, gentle souls so full of grace,
A love so pure, no words could ever trace.
So let us celebrate these Yorkshire stars,
With love and admiration that truly mars,
All other breeds, for in their hearts we find,
A love that's boundless, forever intertwined.

THIRTY-TWO

SUNSHINE'S
GOLDEN RAY

In Yorkshire's realm, a tiny wonder dwells,
With fur as soft as whispers, tales it tells.
The Yorkshire Terrier, a petite delight,
A love that sparkles in the moonlit night.

Eyes like gems, reflecting love divine,
A heart so pure, a spirit that will shine.
In every wag of its tail, a joyful dance,
A bond so strong, it's like a second chance.

With every bark, a song of love it sings,
A melody that echoes through the springs.
Its loyalty, a fortress, steadfast and true,
A companion that will never bid adieu.

In gardens green, it frolics and it plays,
A joyous soul, in sunshine's golden rays.

A guardian of hearts, a guardian of souls,
A love that fills the void, makes us whole.
 It snuggles close, with warmth it does bestow,
A Yorkshire Terrier, a love that overflows.
In gentle paws, a love that never wanes,
A bond unbreakable, through all life's pains.
 Oh, Yorkshire Terrier, a love divine,
In your embrace, the world is made benign.
Forever cherished, forever by our side,
A love that in our hearts will e'er abide.

THIRTY-THREE

LOYALTY UNMATCHED

In a world of boundless joy, a Yorkshire Terrier's grace,
With fur of gold and eyes so bright, a love I can't replace.
A tiny frame, a heart so pure, a spirit that's unchained,
My love for them, forever deep, will never be restrained.
Their paws so dainty, like delicate blooms, they dance upon the floor,
A playful skip, a joyful leap, their energy does soar.
With loyalty unmatched, they stay close by, a constant, loving friend,
Through life's ups and downs, they'll be there until the very end.
Their yaps like music, a symphony of joy, a melody

so sweet,
Their presence fills my heart with warmth, a love that can't be beat.
With eyes that gleam with boundless love, they melt away my fears,
In their embrace, I find solace, a haven through the years.

Their tiny bodies hold a soul so fierce, a warrior within,
They face the world with courage strong, their spirit won't give in.
Though small in size, their love grows large, filling up my days,
With each wag of their tail, my heart swells, lost in their loving gaze.

So here's to Yorkshire Terriers, the angels in disguise,
With love so pure, they bring us joy, a precious gift in our lives.
Their presence brightens every day, their love knows no bounds,
In their tiny frames, a love so big, forever it resounds.

THIRTY-FOUR

OUR YORKSHIRE TERRIER FRIENDS

In a world of tiny creatures,
With hearts so pure and true,
There's a breed that steals our hearts,
The Yorkshire Terrier, oh so few.

With their silky coats of gold and blue,
And eyes that sparkle like the sky,
Yorkies bring joy to me and you,
With every wag and playful sigh.

They prance around with regal grace,
Their presence fills the room,
Their love, a gentle embrace,
Bringing light amidst the gloom.

Their loyalty knows no bounds,
Their spirit, brave and bold,

In their tiny paws, love resounds,
More precious than silver or gold.
    They cuddle close upon our laps,
Their warmth, a soothing balm,
Their tiny yips, like gentle taps,
A symphony of love and calm.
    With hearts full of endless zeal,
They brighten up our days,
Their love, a love that's real,
In their presence, worries fade away.
    So let us celebrate these little gems,
Our Yorkshire Terrier friends,
For in their eyes, love never ends,
A bond that forever transcends.

ABOUT THE AUTHOR

Walter the Educator is one of the pseudonyms for Walter Anderson. Formally educated in Chemistry, Business, and Education, he is an educator, an author, a diverse entrepreneur, and the son of a disabled war veteran. "Walter the Educator" shares his time between educating and creating. He holds interests and owns several creative projects that entertain, enlighten, enhance, and educate, hoping to inspire and motivate you.

Follow, find new works, and stay up to date
with Walter the Educator™
at www.WaltertheEducator.com

Milton Keynes UK
Ingram Content Group UK Ltd.
UKHW020638140923
428670UK00014B/556